Praise for *500 Sentences*

A wonderful list poem containing self-reflective, contemplative, humcrous, and tragic lines— essentially koans on the realities of modern and timeless existence. A perfectly enjoyable immersion into an ouroboros philosophy!
  Alice Burdick, author of *Flutter* and *Deportment*

A sentence always begins with a capital letter and ends with a period. Difficult to make anything of that, it would seem.

Usually a sentence is part of a larger idea, moving along to the next one and then the one after and then another forming a paragraph. Not usually left on its own for one to consider. So when left alone, just sat there, the need of drama, humour, a truth or some other possibility waiting to continue would be usual.

And 500 of them, which over a period of years have arrived in my inbox, have given me a daily thought, a brief idea to think on.

There are many that I've collected for later use, you might say stolen. Some passed along to others to brighten their day. There are favourites depending on what the day might be, what that day's brief "poem" suggests...

  After a dream like that, the following day becomes a fcotnote.

Mistaking your country for the world and mistaking the world for everything are the same mistake.

Bill Smith, author, musician, filmmaker, photographer, publisher

If there are ever 500 sentences to read, these are they. The author speaks to who he is: "Our experiences don't define who we are; who we are defines our experiences."

Through the lens of a poet, artist, musician, philosopher, historian, environmentalist and much more, Artur Bull imbues these 500 sentences with insightful revelations about the beauty as well as contradictions in life. While each sentence is independent, together they are interdependent and speak to some of the gravest injustices of our time: oppression, land dispossession, slavery, and climate change.

At the same time, *500 Sentences* also reveals observations in relation with animal and fish relatives and the ecologies in which we all live, while exposing our fragilities of being human, including the ups and downs of love.

After all, "I'm pretty sure this is the full immersion program."

Sherry Pictou, member and former Chief of L'sɨtkuk First Nation, District Chief for Confederacy of Mainland Mi'kmaq, Associate Professor, Dalhousie University.

500 Sentences
© 2024 Arthur Bull

Cover design: Rebekah Wetmore
Editor: Andrew Wetmore

ISBN: 978-1-998149-52-0
First edition June 2024

MOOSE HOUSE
PUBLICATIONS

2475 Perotte Road
Annapolis County, NS
B0S 1A0

moosehousepress.com
info@moosehousepress.com

We live and work in Mi'kma'ki, the ancestral and unceded territory of the Mi'kmaw People. This territory is covered by the "Treaties of Peace and Friendship" which Mi'kmaw and Wolastoqiyik (Maliseet) People first signed with the British Crown in 1725. The treaties did not deal with surrender of lands and resources but in fact recognized Mi'kmaq and Wolastoqiyik (Maliseet) title and established the rules for what was to be an ongoing relationship between nations. We are all Treaty people.

Also by Arthur Bull

and available from Moose House Publications

Foreword

As the title suggests, this book consists of five hundred sentences. I initially was going to call them aphorisms, but changed my mind because I wanted to avoid any association with the bumper-sticker sayings that fill social media. Besides, many of the sentences are not aphorisms.

Likewise, 'maxims' seemed to call up the witty writing of the classic 18th century writers like La Rochefoucauld, which were a little too sharply clever for what I needed. Then I considered 'one-line poems', or even 'one-line prose poems', but this seemed too much like generic hair-splitting. I even thought of 'Sententia', but found out that Peter Lombard snagged this title in the 12th century.

The basic problem was how to write sentences without becoming sententious. So I ended up with this most factual of titles.

I wrote these sentences as a daily practice, four a day for more than a year, and then posted them on my blog. This diaristic process began in March 2023, when I bought a collection of one-sentence poems called *Voices*, by Argentinian poet Anronio Porchia, in a used bookstore in Bangkok. This sparked the beginning of a daily ritual, which I shared with a small but select group of readers.

This is the first time I have written in this form, that is, using the sentence as the poetic structural frame, but I soon realized that I had joined a very long and distinguished body of creators of one-sentence literature that stretches from Confucius to Kafka and beyond.

Although the sentences are arranged in no particular sequence or narrative, there are thematic undercurrents that connect them in a rhizome-like way, for anyone who wants to look.

I would like to thank the dedicated circle of readers who were part of daily sharing of sentences. Their attention and their wonderful responses made this such an enjoyable journey.

Arthur Ball
May, 2024

For Sam and Ippei

Arthur Bull

500 Sentences

Arthur Bull

I tried to pay attention but got distracted by my attention.

I started with either, but now I lean towards neither, or neither.

Worried about how to fill my long day, I filled it with worry.

It's just a matter of time, he said, assured of his grip on both time and matter.

Luckily, I don't have to judge anyone until I am appointed to the bench.

Indifference and difference aren't that different.

Arthur Bull

There's no going within without going without.

Of all the modes of human consciousness, surely our daily waking consciousness is the most bossy.

What you don't know holds up what you know.

I wouldn't go so far as to say anything that needed going far to be said.

I bought a ticket for an ensemble production, but it turned out to be a one-man show.

Whatever put the Butte in beauty also put the fur in furniture.

Why do the people in charge of security always make me feel insecure?

The familiar margin between my lack and my need got overgrown with weeds, so now it's a green zone.

As if that weren't enough, we still weren't able to find out how much was enough.

I am breaking up my heart into smaller, more manageable pieces.

He wasn't looking forward to his rendezvous with the physical world.

After a dream like that, the following day becomes a footnote.

The difficulty of the ending and the difficulty of the beginning were difficult to tell apart.

Arthur Bull

The arrangement of everyone's comings and goings had a finality that always seemed a bit much.

The slide down and the climb up cover the same distance.

We were not taught much about fundamentals, except that they were fundamental.

A starting pistol only targets the runners.

Memory is like a pet python: to be trusted, but only up to a point.

Atonement without attunement is just alignment.

A book called *The New Poetry* is instantly old.

Resistance is to electricity what dissent is to politics.

Instinct is deep intention; intention is shallow instinct.

Mistaking your country for the world and mistaking the world for everything are the same mistake.

I know what I believe, but I'm not sure I believe what I know.

Guilt is to shame as fire is to water.

History: a spiral-shaped corkscrew.

There is no artificial wisdom.

Arthur Bull

Never send a kiss by messenger.

Airports need high ceilings to hold all the emotions.

Sovereignty excludes the sovereign.

You can go further back, and you can go further forward, but can you go further into here and now?

The marriage between the Law and the Truth wasn't always easy.

You didn't know it, then you did, then you didn't again.

The beavers' moral code may be different than ours.

War is mostly not a time of happiness, except for warriors.

Belief and doubt together form a perfect figure-eight.

Law is to truth as aspiration is to desire.

Against the rough winds of the world, my body would be frail and vulnerable without its necessity.

Unburdened by talent, I carry on.

Stepping out of a dream is one thing; stepping back in is another.

The means of production are produced by the production of means.

Arthur Bull

The flash of consciousness is invisible in sunlight.

Now that there is no longer an 'away', where exactly is 'here'?

Their anger often led them to mistake the limit of their critical faculties for articles of faith.

You can fight fire with fire, or fire with water, but you can't fight water with water.

The economy of grievance always has a deficit.

When you finally got what you wanted, you realized that it was not at all final.

It was a relief to finally reach the point of no return.

Stylish but expensive is common.

There are many ways of knowing there are many ways of knowing.

The pleasure is in the texture.

Filled with certainty: the headstone of a famous general.

And a special thank you to the material world for providing light acccmpaniment.

It is not important to be important.

Good conversations keep going.

Arthur Bull

You can't have an accident by mistake.

If the rest is history, what came before the rest?

Bronze bells melted down for weapons still ring.

If everyone would just be like us, things would be easier.

Explaining the physical attributes concurrent with a phenomenon does not exhaust our understanding of it.

Everything but remains remain.

The last scene switches from black-and-white to colour.

The only thing is the only thing.

What people think of you isn't really an interesting topic.

Words are not shadows (unless you put them in brackets).

Every character is a character.

Eyes are for both seeing and crying.

Some emotions have no names.

Nation states are temporary fictions, and we should make the most of them.

Arthur Bull

Predators fall prey.

Forgotten memories can't be forgotten.

To make a word into a thing, put it in *italics*.

A good explanation was turned back at the border.

I was waiting patiently for my impatience to subside.

Misery is just the hard edge of happiness.

That sheen the world gives off *is* the world.

What goes on goes off; what goes off goes on.

We lost so much that when we won we thought we'd lost.

So was another day added or subtracted?

I don't know much, but I like what I know.

Who will protect us from our protectors?

Is it useless to understand the use of uselessness?

The sound of each word casts its shadow.

All our mistakes are truthful.

Kicking yourself does not make you go faster.

Arthur Bull

Even though good intentions have a bad name, they are still good.

If you have an impoverished view of the human mind, your replica of the human mind will also be impoverished.

Did anyone really think that the mind was only for thinking?

Words are reservoirs where versions collect.

We had an argument, but we had to let it go because it was too expensive to keep.

This is enough; that was enough.

When it comes to theories of death, some like it straight and some like it round.

You only need enough technique to create what you want to create, and the rest is baggage.

The future perfect will have been long gone by then.

Something always falls into place, like it or not.

Even though it stays still, the bridge crosses the river; even though it is moving, the river doesn't cross the bridge.

Children may be little, but their worlds are bigger than it will ever be again.

One kiss can change everything.

The gap between the event and the story keeps widening.

Arthur Bull

There is no point in being a part because a point has no part apart.

Slavery wounds all humanity.

Rhythms, like waves, are circular.

Some circles have entrances and exits, and some are closed.

In the countryside a siren means something different.

Is the essential essential?

Maybe better to lose your edge than lose your surface.

If these arrangements were natural there would be no natural.

The boots of power don't always fit.

A world with no domination is just one step away.

We all understand how to use the useful, but not many know how to use the useless.

I dreamed I was canoeing with Sinead O'Connor.

We could refuse to be programmed.

You are not as happy, or as unhappy, as you think you are.

Arthur Bull

There is something compelling about religion.

It wasn't an explanation that made the white clouds white.

Strong convictions aren't famous for their nuance.

Art adds space.

Learning requires unlearning.

It's reciprocal: you are being transformed by me, and I am being transformed by you.

Losing control was more attractive in theory.

Happiness and unhappiness have one thing in common: neither has an on/off switch.

The first thing to do when taking someone's land is to say they are not there.

Events make patterns, even if you can't see them.

Justice is a perennial: the more it gets cut back, the more it grows.

Let's start tomorrow: that mountain isn't going anywhere.

You don't have to join; it turns out you are already a member.

Arthur Bull

To examine your own opinions, first detach them, then look at them, then replace them and see if they fit.

Their personalities were the least interesting thing about them.

The departed are characters in an endless production.

If you live in an empire, try not to call it an empire.

Each time you get lost anywhere is a version of the first time you got lost somewhere.

Through the torn fabric of history we got a glimpse of who we might have been.

Music is not sport.

Predicates are a dime a dozen.

Temporality will be restored momentarily.

A world where everything is accounted for counts for nothing.

Letting go is also love.

They cherished their freedom and chose the wrong path, the one that leads to slavery.

Practising without practice is impracticable.

The yellow warblers seem to have cracked The Problem of Style.

Arthur Bull

He had tumbled upon the class of things that could not exist in any possible world.

Some foods, like baseball hotdogs or cold baked beans, rely on connotation more than denotation.

Some worry that there is no meaning to life, and some worry there is too much.

What could be clearer than not knowing?

The stuff in the lost and found office was mostly just lost, because when something was found it was no longer there.

The shed carapace of a moulting lobster is an exact replica of its own body.

What is not incomplete?

And, before you know it, you will have mastered the art of being lost.

If you could see length, width and height unattached to anything, that would hold everything.
'Is it hopeless?' is the most hopeful of questions.

You can stop beginning now.

If we are all headed for disaster, why are we racing?

Loneliness is not having someone to tell that you are lonely.

The authentic is a recent innovation.

Once you get the approval you are seeking, what will you to do with it?

Arthur Bull

Arrested on charges of unemployment, I immediately gave up the names of my co-conspirators, including Zhuangzi, Andy Marvell, Seneca the Elder and Chuck Berry.

If you don't want someone to repeat something, don't tell them.

If you think you already know everything you need to know about someone without having met them, then you know less than you think you know.

The announcement said *There will be a temporary delay*, as though there were any other kind.

What I imagine what I want is never what I imagine is enough.

The something missing isn't what I missed; it's what I might miss, missing this.

Some mistakes are only ornamental.

Some possibilities don't come with a description.
The courtroom is not a place of peace.

It's good to learn another animal language.

A definition is by definition a definition.

We barely scratched the surface, but I think we should send it for re-polishing anyway.

As well as everything else it is, a sentence is also a melody.

Experience was waiting patiently for a chance to speak.

Arthur Bull

Opinions make good anchors, but they need to be hauled before you go anywhere.

Where are the conspiracy people when you need them?

No one really knows how to slow down the inflation of language.

Two hopeless people together: unstoppable

It wasn't the music that was sacred; it was the audience.

Breaking your own rules and breaking the law both come with penalties, one private and one public.

Beauty is always a greeting.

Listen: beneath the chatter of voices, there's a steady hum of people losing people.

Some are climbing, some are trying not to fall, some are falling.

Due to interference by events, today's hiatus has been cancelled.

If you almost drowned in Lake Erie, that is how you will always think of it.

We may not all be refugees, but we all need refuge.

'Of course I can drive a car. I'm not a poet.'

Some words float, some sink; either way, they make ripples.

Arthur Bull

Small engine repair is always useful, and sometimes essential.

His relationship with the physical world was often strained.

Extremely unlikely pays best odds.

Quality has no quantity.

Uncooperative, words, often to obey, refuse.

You'll know when a flood stops being a metaphor.

Listen to the unheard.

What I thought was here for good is gone, and what I thought was gone for good is here.

Mind the mind.

I thought it was the Streamline, but it was the B&O.

Their story was inscribed in the ancient calligraphy of creases and wrinkles.

He traced the genealogy of possible worlds in the dirt with a stick.

What I was thinking about it was not what I thought I thought I was thinking about it.

The best dives make the least splash.

Arthur Bull

If you try to discuss meaning, your discussion will soon end up being meaningless.

Many sentences want to begin a novel, but very few are chosen.

Pay close attention to kindness wherever you find it.

Democracy means closing the circle and then breaking it open again.

Notwithstanding there was little wherewithal whatsoever, we continued to attempt forthwith what had been heretofore impossible.

Anger can open the door to justice, but it can't go through.

Intelligence: sometimes a shield, sometimes a sword, sometimes a lamp.

Symbolic change could be a step toward real change, or a step away from it.

The morning star and the evening star are the same star.

The future perfect will be needed to say that this will have been a long day.

What we thought we did, what we said we did and what we did were all different.

Stories follow events, which follow stories.

There is no conventional wisdom.

Arthur Bull

Thinking you know a lot usually means you know less than you think you know.

He had an amazing capacity to know what he thought about anything before experiencing it.

Here is somebody just like me, with exactly the same birth and death.

Sometimes a wooden horse is just a wooden horse.

Here we are together: there must be a reason.

Democracy is like a bed: you make it in the morning and ruin it at night.

Composition radiates outward from experience.

It can be hard to see how easy it is.

Rhetorical questions necessarily fold in on themselves.

The climb over our own preconceptions was often steep and hard.

Those repressed emotions were bucked, split, stacked, and ready for winter.

Thoughts, words and actions are translucent.

Hurtful words come from wordless hurt at the heart of words.

The Oracle told him that he will meet her in this life, but that he will not recognize her.

Arthur Bull

The variable rate of the unravelling added variety.

They somehow knew they were in each other's thoughts.

The forest is medicine.

Beginning again usually requires beginning again again.

Genealogy is the nervous system of history.

Wishing someone a happy death is not considered good manners.

You can't see sight.

Making an excuse and making a birdhouse both create accommodation.

We are all part of something bigger, or something smaller.

Apparently you can give up on yourself, give yourself up and give yourself away all at the same time.

Unburdened by talent, I go where I please.

The ocean has no liquidity.

The present will be presented presently.

Do beavers have property rights?

It's the other thyme that heals all things.

Philosophy is catch-and-release.

The present is a door that is always open and always closed.

Airports have high ceilings to hold the strong emotions.

They advise that the subjunctive be used subjectively.

Formalize the informal just enough to form form.

Poetry is smash-and-grab.

Any similarity to any narrative, real or imagined, is purely coincidental.

I bow down to Joe Pie Weed.

When subordinate clauses become insubordinate, full-out mutiny cannot be far behind.

To call a chicken a Meat King adds a double insult to that creature's injury.

My expectations were not too high; they were just too detailed.

The biology of history includes the history of biology.

Happiness is not a puzzle; it is a practise.

Arthur Bull

The rhythm of the alternation between being lost and being found is unpredictable.

Having exhausted all options. I lay down in the shade of an apple tree.

Some are called; some call; some both; and some neither.

While investigating the source of an impulse, he stumbled upon a series of smaller obsessions.

Sometimes one glimpse of a smile is exactly enough.

They believed they could make make-believe into belief simply by believing.

Sea monkeys are an underutilized species.

It's not hard to keep a secret if you have the stamina.

No need to worry about death: that's all been taken care of.

The female roles were played by boys, and the boys' roles were played by women.

Her smile was like putting your feet in the lake after a long walk.

Emotional confessions should be spread out.

He had the ability to invent, solve and forget a crisis in a single morning.

If an egg is stuck to the carton it might be broken, in this and all possible worlds.

Arthur Bull

Your happiness will not fly on the wings of someone else's unhappiness.

Some days, it's life that's long and art that's short.

There is no solution to the mind-body problem because there is no problem.

They unloaded a new shipment of outcomes to be distributed across the country.

You can keep rehearsing for past performances, but you will never improve on them.

We are to each other dreams of other dreams.

I have given the birds permission to eat my blackberries.

On reaching the unknowable again they made up another story.

All endings are beginnings.

I wonder how big a role we have in the mythology of birds.

Beavers have organized their labour differently.

My dreams must have been like glaciers, judging by the landscape of my bedclothes.

Although I was not made to, I made up something to be made into something I want.

If a policy seems misguided, check to see who is guiding it.

Arthur Bull

Department store diners had glossy plastic menus with colour photos of the food.

I forget who I was trying to impress.

The relations between the sentences are hidden from view.

The beavers are sleeping it off after a long night of gnawing and hauling.

Some permits are non-renewable.

Nor are the so-called wise gods more reliable than winged dreams.

The road in and the road out are the same road.

Something is the matter if nothing but matter matters.

we sorted our memories as good, bad or neutral, as though that were an important thing to do.

A crew was sent out to clear away the last remaining exceptions.

'It was meant to be' was not meant to be.

There is no such thing as an unlimited right.

I lost my balance and nearly fell into quandary.

Belief and doubt together form a perfect figure-eight.

Arthur Bull

I turned on the Memory Channel but it was all re-runs.

You can't take in more than you can take, but you can make what you can take in more.

The effects of the hurricane as of more interest to us than their causes.

Laid out, the sequence of events made a floral pattern.

'Who do you think you are?' implies that who you are has anything to do with who you think you are.

Wish fulfillment was the most productive sector of the economy.

Oppression trains the oppressed to be oppressors.

It was problematic, but it wasn't a problem.

Just because there is an EXIT sign doesn't mean you have to leave.

Rules for talking to yourself: 1) always use the reflexive pronoun; 2) make sure you are alone.

Symphonies are like sailing ships.

The very word 'subjugate' inflicts violence on a sentence.

There is no romance in romanticizing.

No one gets to chcose where they are born.

Arthur Bull

People who know something easily forget what it is like not to know.

The search for happiness was called off, and the crews given a well-deserved rest.

The lake held its stories the way it held its sunlight.

I can take my chances, but I can't keep them.

All the particles were attracted to the 'the'.

Everywhere he looked, he saw the word 'should'.

It can be difficult being an expat from another world.

There was either too much transparency or not enough.

You can't store happiness.

It's nothing, we say, or it's everything, when we know it's neither.

Should always lands with a thud.

If you think the mind is a thinking machine, then the thinking machine that you think up will look a lot like a mind to you.

Some sentences fragments.

You have had quite a bit of success, considering that you are not even dead yet.

Arthur Bull

The name of a note is its least important feature.

Experiencing experience and listening to listening are the same thing.

The wave that's coming behind this wave is already here.

Anxiety and worry claim to be in charge, but in fact they are quite junior.

Ancestor worship is fine, descendant worship even better.

The ineffable includes the effable.

Between connotation and denotation flowed a little brook.

The comedy of greed often goes unnoticed.

Love, like whiskey, is good even though it is bad for you.

I yelled, "Don't break," to the glass as it fell through the air.

Some misfits are too loose, some are too tight.

Dinosaurs are modern.

Tidal rivers contradict themselves.

Dusk reminds the day of dawn.

A learning curve is a section of a learning circle.

Arthur Bull

There isn't just one Bo Diddley beat.

To make a verb infinite, use the infinitive.

The memory of love is a red leaf reflected on water.

The resurrection of the body seems like a radical solution.

To find the volume of a word first measure its circumference.

I am beholden to everyone I've held.

Tautology is tautology.

The poets of the Late Tang did not know It was the Late Tang.

No walls, no gate.

The cost of their great achievements was a debt deferred.

Unshakable beliefs obscure the view.

Our experiences don't define who we are; who we are defines our experiences.

I was never confused about it until they asked me to describe it.

A lightbulb is not an example of light.

Arthur Bull

The inside story is always inside another story.

A group of women with umbrellas were crossing a bridge in a light rain.

Alignment without attunement is confinement.

Roots don't grow in the past.

The chronological is only one way to arrange events.

You thought the very things you thought weren't the things you didn't think.

The expression is in the variation.

Remedies for infirmity of mind may include purgatives, cordials, alternatives, corroboratives, and tentatives.

Her dance was as slow as the moon crossing the sky.

Surrounded by new implications, she picked one and put it in a vase.

Autumn has begun to take down the decorations.

You don't need to be sleeping close by to visit someone's dreams.

1967: Expo was in Montréal, the Cup was in Toronto and love was in the air.

Ordinary activities are good painkillers but can become addictive.

Arthur Bull

I'm pretty sure this is the full immersion program.

Their plan to undo past wrongs using money and violence seemed a little far-fetched.

My art, my rules.

Words are always used in their broadest sense.

At night cathedral windows are black.

Some sequences are irreversible: fetch egg, cook egg, eat egg.

It was foreseen that foreground would be foregone.

I used to think I was giving voice to the trees; now I see that the trees are giving voice to me.

Tattoos and drugs: some cultures handle them better than others.

The optical inversion from black-figure to red-figure was the figure for the embodiment of awakening.

To leave and enter the world at the same time, use the same door.

If the meaning is clear, it is transparent; if the meaning is transparent, you can see through it; if you can see through it, what are you looking at?

November's bare branches are now filled with red, yellow, orange and pink memories.

Arthur Bull

Stale emotions go in the compost.

In the stratigraphy of a word, carefully dig through the layers of time to look for artifacts of meaning.

If I knew I was going to be the sole witness, I would have requested a better memory.

The time it took you to read this sentence is inseparable from this sentence.

More is not less much less more.

Walmart is introducing parking places for the broken-hearted.

I don't know and I don't want to know, although I also don't want not to know.

They said it was anthropomorphism but I thought it was zoomorphism.

Melody desires rhythm.

Only up to a point he said, when really meant up to a line.

You can relegate, delegate, prevaricate, abdicate, abrogate, obfuscate and annotate as much as you want, but sooner or later you're gonna have to regulate.

Beauty creates.

Farewell for now, cove, woodlot, lake, and home.

The body never was an object.

Arthur Bull

The rate of the unravelling may vary, but the direction does not.

In a steam engine, the least powerful and most essential component is the governor.

You can't put out a fire with a sword.

If you are passing by my place, please check in on my hungry crows.

The water needed to put out this raging fire must be drawn from a deep well.

The archaeology of windows lets in new light.

Nothing ventured, nothing lost.

In people, as in diamonds, the internal refection, refraction and dispersal of light increase with the number of facets.

The left left.

What exactly is your identity identical with?

His funeral instructions were simple: just think of the moments of happiness we shared.

I fell asleep in a library and awoke on a ferry.

Pack only what is essential: a bridge, a river, a mountain.

The distance voices of children, the small flashing green light and the raindrops were exactly synchronized.

Arthur Bull

Certainly, what's certain is the certainty of uncertainty.

To say that cityscapes are cubist, that is, monochrome compositions on a flat surface, seems redundant.

Some opinions are load bearing, some just ornamental.

Cats continue their ongoing work on the problem of Other Minds.

Learning circles circle learning circles.

The shoreline sounds with promises and waves.

The difference between yours and ours is why.

Pain keeps you on the surface of your experience, and puts you in the depth of others'.

Sock, cock, lock, dock and rock all have more than one meaning.

Every cell in your body says yes.

Believing is seeing.

Keep going until you feel you are out of your depth, then begin your work.

Reduplication reduplicates.

The alternation between solution and dissolution needs no resolution.

Arthur Bull

I'm never sure whether it's whence or whither.

Auguries told by yarrow stalks twitch between my fingers.

Good memories are medicine.

Peering over the tops of our trenches, we caught a glimpse of each other.

Every act comes complete with its own accountability.

The difference between yours and ours is only why.

Every cell in your body says yes.

Some layers are transparent, some translucent and some just plain opaque.

Believing is seeing.

Keep going until you feel you are out of your depth, then begin your work.

Artful retreat is the hardest manoeuvre.

It seems unlikely that a remedy for past suffering would be future suffering.

They made an intricate pattern of their harsh words and tender moments.

Occasionally, surprised, my body steps into an exact replica of itself.

Arthur Bull

Zealots are known more for their anger than for their insight.

I have a thousand ways to be an idiot, but loving you isn't one of them.

This sentence has three subjects: waves on the river, a heron skimming, a fish jumping.
Blake saw this coming.

All those things you didn't notice are still waiting for you to return.

In the last days, good governance became more important than ever.

Being lost is a prerequisite.

If the weight of the wrongs done to you is not heavy enough, you can add the weight of resentment.

Accept the magic and look to where it is pointing you.

Fingertips touch strings as though for the first time.

Untold stories haunt unlikely places.

Novelists are interested in many people; poets only one...or, if they're lucky, two.

There's no rule that says we always have to choose sides.

What is the difference between curtains and windows?

Arthur Bull

She liked to end her sentence with commas,

While straining our eyes to see the perfect beyond, we missed the perfect here.

Our bones are drums.

I remember the crows rising in my window, forming a pattern I hadn't learned yet.

Attachment to blame and love of justice are not the same thing.

Underestimation of people makes the world smaller.

Learning requires letting go of who you thought you were.

Although they thought they were receiving, they were mostly sending.

Returning follows turning.

It would be easier to see the future if all these hopes and fears weren't in the way.

Consider it considerate.

Everyone brought their own container.

The final word was smudged by a teardrop.

Jack o'Diamonds is a hard card to play.

Composing is composting.

Arthur Bull

A breeze dispersed your reflection.

Even the sovereignty of grief will dissolve.

Hopelessness isn't any more dependable than hope.

There is a spiral where the lines converge.

I do think I think about what I think they think of me, or if they think of me.

The governor's power often outran his judgment.

Your story isn't just what happened to you.

What used to be hard is now easy; what used to be easy is now hard.

Don't assume.

One world ends, another begins.

There is no event that does not resonate.

Belief and doubt together form a perfect figure-eight.

When I dreamed I was dreaming I was awake.

Without preconceptions, noise becomes sound.

Finding the perfect skipping stone is only the first part.

I found out my body was keeping secrets from me.

Arthur Bull

We know about hanging on for dear life, but what about letting go for dear life?

You'd be surprised too if you found out that island you landed on was someone's bald head.

One tiny footprint on a sandbar decodes a lifetime.

I received the message long after the messenger had left.

Opinion is only the tip of the iceberg.

The solution was harder to solve than the problem.

Failure and success were a famous comedy team.

What went before afterwards came behind.

As it turned out, he was all bark and no tree.

Technique that is not essential to the work at hand is excess baggage.

We exchanged our versions of each other.

We preferred peace, order and pretty well anything else.

For easeful rest, add a sliver of moonlight.

Arthur Bull

Are seeing forward and remembering dreams the same thing?

He switched from a solid-body to a hollow-body.

The calligraphy on the walls indicated a building slated for demolition.

The drowning man suddenly realized that this flood was no myth.

For a celebration of human weakness, you need to hire a good band.

Arthur Bull

About the author

Arthur Bull lives in Lake Midway on Digby Neck, in Nova Scotia. He has published eight books of poetry and five chapbooks, and his poems and translations from classical Chinese have appeared in numerous Canadian, US and international journals. He is also a musician and has  been part of the improvised music scene in Canada for more than 40 years.

As a long-time activist he has worked primarily with small-scale fisheries organizations and rural development organizations at the local, national and international level.